13.95-11.16

What's Silly?

by Niki Yektai

illustrated by Susannah Ryan

Clarion Books

New York

Clarion Books
a Houghton Mifflin Company imprint
52 Vanderbilt Avenue, New York, NY 10017
Text copyright © 1989 by Helene Niki Yektai
Illustrations copyright © 1989 by Susannah Ryan
All rights reserved.

For information about permission to reproduce
selections from this book, write to Permissions,
Houghton Mifflin Company, 2 Park Street, Boston, MA 02108.
Printed in the USA

Library of Congress Cataloging-in-Publication Data
Yektai, Niki.
What's silly? / by Niki Yektai; illustrated by Susannah Ryan.
p.   cm.
Summary: The reader follows a family through a whole day of
unusual situations and tries to identify what is silly in each illustration.
ISBN 0-89919-746-9: $12.95 (est.)
1. Literary recreations. [1. Literary recreations.] I. Ryan,
Susannah. ill. II. Title.
PZ7.Y376Wh   1989   88-22883
[E]—dc19   CIP
AC

H 10 9 8 7 6 5 4 3 2 1

For Nicolina Curcio,
her children,
her grandchildren,
and her great-grandchildren.

—N.Y.

_____

For Grandma and Granny

—S.R.

Something is silly.

The SKIRT!

What's silly now?

The SHAVING CREAM!

Now what's silly?

The HAT and DOG!

Something is silly.

The TREES!

What is silly?

The NEST and HAT!

What's silly here?

The KETCHUP and COMB!

Now what's silly?

The CAR and BOAT!

Something is very silly.

The BATHROOM and TV !

Now what's silly?

The FLOWERS and SPAGHETTI!

What's silly here?

The DISHES and SHOES!

What is silly?

The DOG and BABY!

What's silly outside?

The STARS and MOON!

What's silly inside?

The SHEETS and BLANKETS!

That's better. Good night!

Not quite!